PRAISE FOR

MW01168695

Carol Bindel's p
Everyday Poems" but they are everyday like dawns and sunsets.
Some of the poems are about doing farm chores; many are about
family relationships; all of them have a deep awareness of nature
by someone who is well acquainted with it. She is not just a
superficial suburbanite who lives for the TV show Dancing with
the Stars. Her poems dance with the real stars. Her poems come
forth from the floor of her soul and speak directly to God, the
Universe, All That Is. However, she is rooted on this earth. She
herself has summed up the quality of her poetry and her being
in these three lines of her poem, "Survivors": *The most perfected
lives,/ Kiln-fired by sorrow,/ Grow tender, gracious, serene.*

DAN CUDDY, Poet and Editor of the Loch Raven
Review.

Carol has that rare gift of seeing simple truth in the natural,
every day experience. She lifts up what most of us miss in our
rush to get on to the next thing. Her lovingly crafted poems call
us to slow down, pay attention, notice the messages the world
has to offer. Reading one of Carol's poems, one is left feeling
comforted in the recognition of the truth of her words and
challenged to look more closely at our own life experiences.
Carol's wisdom, expressed so beautifully through her poetry, is
a gift to us all.

BETH WOOD-ROIG, Seminarian, Lancaster Theological
Institute

As a long-time admirer of Carol Bindel's poems, I am thrilled to see a volume of her exceptional work in print. Hers is a work of spirit, and of soul, and of the earthly human form that conjoins them. Her words carry me down to the bedrock of myself and my own experience of this world we inhabit—both the world of leaf and rain and stone, and that of sense and thought and emotion. Her rhythms are those of wind and water, of words both spoken and sung—and of the Word, as heard in spiritual traditions the world over. Praises be for Inherited Estate, and the richness that all who read Carol's words stand to inherit because of it.

DANA KNIGHTEN, Editor, Author, and Therapeutic Writing Facilitator

INHERITED ESTATE
A SONG CYCLE

POEMS BY CAROL BINDEL

**WITH A FOREWORD BY
COLLEEN WEBSTER**

**AND AN AFTERWORD BY
EARL W. MORRIS**

**Trace Hay Publications
Printed by Chapbook Press**

Chapbook Press

Chapbook Press
Schuler Books
2660 28th Street SE
Grand Rapids, MI 49512
(616) 942-7330
www.schulerbooks.com

ISBN 13: 978-1-936243-37-2
ISBN 10: 1-936243-37-7

Trace Hay Publications, 17830, 550 th Avenue, Ames, Iowa, earl@threegfarm.com is a small press that specializes in poetry and fiction by new writers. We cooperate with Chapbook Press and Schuler's Books, 28th Street Grand Rapids, Michigan

DEDICATION

to my family

—intimate, extended, beloved—

how our ripple rings echo out

meet and intersect

break into lovely, complicated patterns

each beautiful face

ACKNOWLEDGEMENTS

This collection would not exist without the persistence of Earl W. Morris. Once, decades ago, when he was my Major Professor and was introducing me to another professor, he said,"This girl can write!" Those words felt like high praise at the time, and they lit a spark in me that has grown and grown. It seems he has not changed his mind, he steps up to publish this book.

Dana Knighten turned her editorial skills and all her ways of knowing to create the flow of this collection. Dana has always encouraged me, and now she adds her flare to shape this work. It would be less than it is without her focused participation and her insights.

Colleen Webster is the only one with whom I studied poetry in a formal, focused way. She is that rare combination, poet and extrovert. She teaches with such heart for both student and subject that her lessons have taken deep root in my life, and enhanced it. Some of these poems came into being specifically under her tutelage.

Many others in my circle of family and friends have been steadfast in encouraging me to believe my writing has merit, and in continuing to say this project is of value. To each of you, thank you. You know how many times I would have backed away. Your ways of nurture have been fundamental. And the list is long. I am humbled by how much you have given me.

Thank you.
Carol Bindel

FOREWORD

In a time when so many of us have forgotten how to hear the insistent call of the returning Kill Deer and have loitered in our own cacophony, the voice of Carol Bindel's poems can woo us back to listen to birds, the distant memories of childhood, and nearer strains of family. In this melodious song cycle, we hear of milking cows, selecting eggs, digging rocks and moving firewood. This is a book of elemental sensuousness, Carol's words giving shape to the seduction of a night sky and the lit windows of a warm kitchen. It is also a recognition of the deeper tones of pain, loss, sorrow--Notes we often chose not to carry with us. And we need all of them right now.

I first came to know Carol in the literary community of our chosen home county, Harford, in Maryland. Her soft but sturdy presence was warming, her quick smile a bit mischievous in a way I later came to associate with her poems; these were words strung together to give a glimpse of a life. As William Blake had his *Songs of Innocence and Experience*, so too, Carol's cycle sings of each.

And she also listens. These poems are testament to the voices that shape us, the ones that specifically shaped Carol's early life, and then echo still today, though as she admits in "Centenary," "I still don't always listen." And that is the lovely tension in this volume. There is blind faith and trust, and then there is practicality and reality that re-shapes the life, that perhaps changes the tune of the singer. Each poem in this book is a stepping-stone along the part of daily struggle. And each is evidence of peace hard-won.

As a college professor who has met with poets in workshop format for 18 years, I can say I have witnessed Carol not only crafting her poems, honing her voice, but listening to her voice as others hear it. She wants her work to reach those who also know struggle, though perhaps in different forms. In that workshop format, I watched her listen carefully to others' voices, linking her attention to the insights of others--an important skill for a writer of any genre.

One of my favorite stories of Carol comes from a time I was teaching her. I ask students to read a book of poetry and respond to it in objective summary, subjective response, then identify professional skills learned as a writer and write what I call an apprentice poem. Carol selected a volume of poetry by Mary Oliver and set to the task in the way only she would. She read, re-read, then typed out the whole volume to really get the words and rhythms of Oliver into her own body. That is the kind of poetry student Carol Bindel is.

She is also that kind of student in life. Nothing is overlooked, undervalued, or discarded. Carol knows that even each washing of a toilet bowl is an opportunity to accept kneeling as prayer. We would all do well to still the chaos in our lives for a bit and listen to the harmonious, jangling and clear-voiced poems she has wrought.

Colleen Webster

PREFACE

A Song Cycle is a series of songs written in one voice. That is, the words of one writer, with music, designed to be performed in a unified sequence. For me, this collection developed into such a sequence. Others helped me to hear my own voice singing a composition that now feels to me like more than the sum of its parts.

These poems were written over two decades. Their roots, though, go back to my girlhood. I am the youngest child of a farmer and a homemaker teacher. My parents were simple people. Simple, that is, in the way that, with deep attention and contemplation, one can hold enormous and difficult complexity, bring clarity to it, and turn it into a way of being that makes a calm, generous and peaceful spirit look easy.

In my unconscious, just-is, childhood years I was immersed in the routines and requirements of farm life, in a large, complicated family and in the all-encompassing social structure of the local Church of the Brethren. It took a long time to sort out some of the details of what was happening under the ordinary-seeming surface of my intricately interconnected growing-up surroundings. Many of these poems reflect parts of that process of maturing perception. I hope my specific songs may evoke for readers their own variations of common life experiences.

The music part is the rhythm and varied tones of the words when spoken. These pieces are to be read aloud, translated from my voice into yours, to be shared as air and breath are shared.

Come, sing with me the songs of our common heritage, songs of our life on this precious earth.

Carol Bindel

CONTENTS

PRELUDE

POND BOTTOM STONE

Pond bottom stone: Smooth, rounded, whole

Sunny surface, and calm.
Glimmering tranquility reigns

One heavy teardrop falls.
Sunbeams shatter, splinter.
Ripple rings expand.
Smooth stone rocks.

Shimmering serenity returns.
Peace again, tear included.

Pond bottom stone: smooth, rounded, whole

I

EMERGENCE

THE IDEA

The Idea,
still just penciled words on a scrap of yellow paper
in her pocket, wrinkled yet crisp between her fingers,

her idea feels weighty and hidden like that rock
revealed in the mud of the footer trench yesterday
at quitting time: size unknown, may need dynamite.

Out on the highway a tractor-trailer
air-horn blast, a demand for attention.
(Her husband? Hooked up, headed north already?)
A train whistle blares and fades.
On the south side, her piano
stands by the wall, silent.

This past hour has gone in mindless routine:
breakfast, lunches, kids out the door. Shower,
dust, do laundry, make beds. It's her day off.

But the smell of fresh coffee suggests new strength
drawn from deep wells. She will try again
to perfect   The Idea   after a cup or two.

DAILY DEVOTION

You began as a thought.
Grandma's hands knew everything.
You never knew her; you are her.
This loud and silent presence,
joined.
You are but a flea,
and its shadow is your loneliness.
Have you lost your roots?
You are not alone.

WELCOME!

step right up
to the strange
scary eye

walk on through
to the rolling blue
green land

bring whatever
gift
you have to give

WALK WITH THE MOON

The bold-faced winter moon
draws cream and charcoal lines,
striking questions and stark lies
where once I imagined I knew
the terrain.

Time and I follow the moon,
step by step, window by window,
entranced, tricked beyond knowing
into her strange forever realm
of light.

FROM DEEP SKIES

Spring entices you, innocent
leaves and petals, and the warm
air whispering hints of freedom.

Summer pulls off your shirt
lays its firey solstice length
on your bare, receptive flesh.

You twirl about, entwined in
the rope of time that pays out
smooth as taffy.

You savor the salty smell
of the sea, of suntan lotion
and fast-food, frying.

You surrender to joy
as a pebble tumbling in
the tidal dance.

Then you get tired of it all,
the heat and hours as dull
as plywood on broken windows.

Then you blink and see children
returning to school, and you,
too, seek renewal from deep

September skies, as torn sheets
of calendar days flutter away
and time coils 'round again.

FINDING BALANCE

In childhood I learned to stride
in free and unconsidered ways
before my lessons.

Mother taught me
to balance a book on my head,
to walk by bending knee, hip, shoulder
level-headed, steady, smooth. She said,

Imagine a thread
from above your crown
through your backbone
to your arches
holding you tall.

Later, learning to walk again,
shuffling, weak, unsteady
behind my blue and black Cruiser DX
posture, movements, balance, all
a conscious, willed effort,

I learned to stand, spine tall,
head level as under that book,
knowing that which holds me up
depends on the strength
of some vibrant, invisible thread.

PERFECT SECRETS

you don't always know
you have enough courage

pain awakes to ride
the night, to search and probe
in places once unknown

ahead the journey
singular

MORNING RUN

She watches glimmers of dawn
blush over tranquil trees, sap-flow-limber
after the stiff rule of winter, standing
there as if posed in party gowns, waiting
for breezes to rise and invite them to dance

as she once waited, feeling bare, limbs
and nubbins on her trunk unmasked by
the fabric of her first party dress, unaccustomed
movements, unpracticed, gawky and awkward
in a body that seemed not to fit
in a sour-smelling, nervous, young place.

As she runs, panting and flushed, she remembers
that heat in her cheeks, the pain of waiting,
immobile, for music, a partner,
whose eyes might affirm her,
erase that homely, paralyzed self,
estranged from the clique and its sway.

Now seasons beyond then, strong
in the dawn, no consort to lead her,
she runs under blossoms and budding leaves,
draws robust breath deep-down sure
of her value, her virtue, her strength,
a woman free at last.

HOW TO FIND YOUR POEM

Awaken in your earthskin.
Rise from your bed
of rocks and thorny roses.
Muck out the horse stall.
Eat blood. Drink pain.
Sweat.

Then stand
as tall as you can.
Reach into the heart
of the sun.
Draw out a handful
of radiance.

II

INNOCENCE

EVERYTHING BUT LIGHT

In a half-dream-before-waking,
little capsules of color
almost like bubbles

dance in dark space
and the Universe trills
so pleased for playfulness

and beauty. Even injured
and disappearing ones are
wholly acceptable.

Rendered in haiku—
within and between
the void and all matter, you,
an ovoid rainbow—

those two words appear
     void
     ovoid

one letter of difference,
only that
circle of potential apart.

I rise into the promise
of day, sunshine flows
from just above the horizon
straight into my eyes.

I lose sight of everything
but light.

FIRSTHAND KNOWLEDGE

Hands filled with knowledge
of work horse coats and muscles

a farm child gazed at her big new school:
office, all-purpose room, ten classrooms
all along a long hall

glint and gleam and brand new shine,
bright passages to glass
doors brilliant with morning light.

Her school-day hallway stretched forever,
radiant path to heaven, she thought.

She thought, studied, traveled.

Flickering monitor face lays claim
to fragile art, collections, books,
things to lay hands on,

wonders guarded by gargoyles
and columns, enormous things
compressed, reduced to pixels

and screens in cubicles,
signals from steel towers
no need for natural

light. Through sealed glass
she searches for sunlight lost

in concrete tunnels in a small world

where amazing turns mundane,
everything shrinks, everyone rushes,
more and more pleases less and less.

She reaches out her hand

EXPLORE BEYOND

fearsome wind and beaten rain
when you calm
yourself to observe

exit doors
in your room of pain
open inward

steps
spiral
as seasons

new plaids of rooms appear
multicolor
flowers in the letter box

EACH SMALL THING

one day's mail to sort: the blessing
of a friendship letter, bills and a way to pay;

one puddle to wipe from the kitchen floor
on my knees for a moment's reflection;

one chair to re-glue, smooth, old,
polished oak once the seat of elders;

one bathtub to clean, remembering
the laughter and fun that left the ring;

one load of laundry for the miracle
mechanical energy that eases the way;

two loaves of bread to bake for the knowledge
of kneaded, elastic strength, and the joy;

one batch of cookies, the lingering scents
and flavors to share, with tea and a chat;

one child with whom to read;
one who grieves and one to listen;

one who celebrates
and one to join the celebration

let me remember each small thing;
each pithy, intentional, meaning-

full life thing.

ROOMS OF TIME

sometimes
the floor plan of time
lays a huge arena

space
to leap, swing
wide, no barriers.

other time-spaces squeeze
as through a slotted spoon
long halls of allotted tasks.

some large rooms,
defined by commitments,
crowd up with boxes of duty

to be sorted, disposed
before the rooms close
in disorder.

in rooms of extreme
agony or bliss
the plane shifts

to vertical; in one
extended instant we
paint memory's mural.

OLD SONGS

I sing old tunes I've known
since before I can remember.

One of my foremothers
wrote these words in pencil
on yellow tablet paper, now brittle
and discovered in a rafter niche:

I shall live my song
and leave it to my children—
those astute biographers—
to trace my crescendos,
diminuendos, fortes,
subitos, staccatos, legatos,
and accent marks.

Only peasant stock ever tended here.
No one important.

It must have been she who played the piano
now gathering dust and rarely heard.

Have I a better choice,
a more essential goal?

I take wax and a soft rag, polish the wood,
raise the lid, caress the keys, lift my voice.

THESE VINTAGE PORTRAITS

We were untried, then, fresh,
in our wedding album pictures.
(Oh my dear, how I miss you.)

In this one I sit with my gaunt but grinning Dad;
a red couch, a dark table, an open canard of cigarettes.
He didn't make it to our wedding.

Here I stand for fitting at the bridal shop—
                          so slender and supple—
and there in the background hangs a gauzy row of veils.
Mirrored, they echo to the mysterious vanishing point.

See the pastor at the church, formal in his collar? Bland
smile, slicked-back hair, high forehead and long nose,
he always reminded me of some angelic dolphin.

There you are before the nuptials with your groomsmen
all so pure in Navy whites.

Mom and me, standing face-to-face, hand-in-hand.
Silent together, how I gazed at some maze of childhood,
the celebrations, indignations, jealousies, and joys
only she knew of me, remembered in her eyes.

Arm in arm Mom and I walk the aisle to you.

No picture shows how, together, you and I dreamed
of life in a nebulous place, a family sufficient, you
an artist, a fine cabinetmaker, me
raising sheep, wool my for spinning. Our dream
discounted realities, amenities. We settled
north of Baltimore. Now our granddaughter

Tip-toes to the lip of adulthood.
Her eyes sparkle, she and I laugh and make fun
of these vintage portraits, paraphernalia
and souvenirs from life's portfolio.

She says, *I'm like you, Gran*, imagines she sees
our existence caught in summation. She doesn't know
the future will bring her clearest views
reflected in her mirror.

LOVE LIKE WATER

I am light like day,
I am love like water
when you look through
to the gleaming bed
that cradles me,

Or see yourself
reflected on
the background sky.
When I am pure I have
no scent, no stain, no grit.

Splash me—
cool on hot feet
for comfort;

Drink me—
clear from the fountain,
Sweet as the hush of peace.

LOVE STORY
after a news report, February 14, 2007

They lie on their sides
hugging, face to face
knees bent, his leg on top
next hers, then his, then hers
his arm reaches to her shoulder
her elbow curls as she leans to him.
Their skeletons show that

their noses likely touched
they shared breath

five or six thousand years ago
when last they lay down together

near what is now
the city of Mantova, Italy.

Archaeological dig team leader
Elena Menotti says that she believes
the two died young
because their teeth are mostly intact
and not worn down.

It can not be easy to die
together, hugging, sheltering
one another, protecting. Yet

if they had lived longer
would he have been angry because the meat spoiled
the crop failed and the fire, they were hungry
and her voice sounded harsh as a crow, cawing?
Would she blame him for the baby's death?
Would he have shouted and stalked away
to the hunt, to his death
under the gorgeous orange-red-purple sunset
would she have wept alone?

INTERLUDE

SONG FOR A CHICKEN

She struts on yellow legs and three scratching toes;
her clean, preened feathers lay shiny and smooth;
her black eyes glitter, her neck arches, proud.
She is yours.
You walk into the house where she and her sisters live
free in straw, where you are known and trusted, you open
your throat and sing, they catch their collective breath
and they sing, too.

When the time comes, you grab a leg quickly,
shift the lady to rest as if nesting on your left arm.
She looks about, calm.
You pass by the tool bench.
Your right hand picks up the sharpened hatchet.
You hold her securely so her neck stretches sideways
over the ragged, stained block.
And innocent eye blinks.
One hard, precise chop.
Blood spurts out.
You watch the headless body dancing to silence.
You remember her song.

III

LOSS

DRINKING WATER

Drinking water from the well
gathers in our holding tank.

The tank is blue
as summer pond water under golden noon
sunshine poured from a cloudless sky.

John, son of Elizabeth and Zechariah, stood
under sky and sun in water's flow,
in the River Jordan, baptizing multitudes,
preaching forgiveness to whoever would come
to drink deep of the One who came after him.

In childhood I played in clear creek water
that tumbled over round brown stones,
then slowed, shallow by my sand bar.
I simply drank when thirsty.
It was safe.

One hot summer day some TV preacher
looked in my face and shouted,
Only the Seal on your forehead
will allow you to stand with the Lamb.
Then I looked in the mirror
and nothing was safe anymore.

Now a pipe inserted as a straw into the earth
brings drinking water to our holding tank.

Hidden. Sealed. Inside in. Outside out.
Perhaps the sealing keeps it pure

TRUST ME THEY SAID

Trust spirals downward
toward black abyss.
He said, she said,
did not, not me,

big-eyed innocence
trips over pain,
doctor whites, funeral flowers,
wretched luscious food smells,

Pine Sol, scrub away
blood stained memory
clings in the crevices
creeps out unaware.

"Let me help," people say.
Break of day, no way.
Alcohol wears off fast,
leaves pretend merry face.

Make believe life is good,
"Don't give up, don't give in,
God's above, all is well,"
people say.

Trust spirals downward.

JULY DROUGHT

moonlight
pins its glare
from a dry
July sky

hot
on wrinkled mud
river bed

hot
as any
parched
and ancient body

pinned
on a wrinkled bed

waiting
waiting
for relief

DRY MOUNTAIN

climb stone steps
through twisted pines

where needles nestle
a snake's tooth

to prick in-
sanity gathered

and disappear
into dry spills

40

GOOD GIRL

Hot, dry tar smell memories
Bible school, "Jesus loves me."
Old, long, dusty lanes
The Book says God and love

Remember?

Hoe the corn and hot, hot sun.
The earth is the Lord's, soil and dirt
and the meek shall inherit

dirt and hurt and hurt all over, hair
roots, fingertips, muscles, joints, soul

tend the kids, tend the laundry,
clean the world and cook and tend.
"Get a job, we need the money."
Straight time, no perks
watch the clock, don't dawdle,
fast and smart, faster, smarter

good girl, jump high, stay
'til they say okay, you may
come down
Please boss
Please papa
Please mama
Please Son
Please...

Dry, hot tar smell
memories

BEWARE, SISTER

One woman's response to Lawrence Ferlinghetti's
"Short Story on a Painting of Gustav Klimt"

Beware, sister,
he is not the one. Look at yourself,

He sways you where you kneel in love's first flowers
on that magical island you imagine together tonight.

His ardent right hand urges you to turn to him;
his left hand possesses your head and neck.

Your right fingers curl, stinging of new,
blinding sensation; you nestle in his thrall.

Your limpid, weakened left hand strokes his right,
your left arm's power vanquished under his cloaked forearm.

His bold harlequined domino hood goes round your
head; the lining spirals gold designs behind your back.

Apollo's laurel wreath crowns his hair; your hair
is sprinkled with star flowers, a nimbus of your mind.

For you, the dangerous black sky and tide fade,
disguised by spattered flecks of his sun-god aura.

His power mounts hectic flags on your cheeks and lips,
your desirous curves melt to him, boneless.

Your ankles and calves— only yours—
are draped with strung heart arrows, sharp points

Embedded in ropy vines to bind, trip,
cripple you when you need to stand.

Your flexed feet and toes— yours alone—
slip off the edge of the earth.

Be wise, dear sister, beware; wait
for your emergent, exquisite self.

DAUGHTER LESSONS

no one cared, then, if you shaved your legs
                —and who knew the possibilities?
or waxed your eyebrows
                see them shine, so clean

Rikers Island, the Museum of Sex,
both unthought of, even
                you needed to learn
how Cain and Able, your crime-fated ova,
betrayed you, but then
                motherhood's pain starts early, ends late

you ate the tempting fruit
                and now we know
you shared with Adam and, joined, you knew
                too much, too little

HOMEGROWN HALF TRUTHS

Tall old man, pride-squared shoulders,
head ringed with a white fringe
like a misplaced, mangy mane. My big
half-brother who looked down on me.

Remember him young? Strong and tough
in a mean world, full of tricks
and how he roared in all the air
so no one nearby had breath to speak.
How he stopped our doors
with "half-" wedges, splinters
pried from family fragments.

His circulation clogged
he lost both legs, then stood
on courage and mid-thigh pegs
and learned to walk again,

and I wondered which half related.
Maybe the torso half, arms akimbo
neck thick and heavy, but not the head
so far above my halfling status.

Or maybe the gut, butt, big old balls
and stumpy stomp-stomp half legs
tamping me down. I had to creep away
before I, too, learned to stand.

WHEN WE MUST STAND

How dare the sun pour forth such golden warmth,
the mountains rise so firm and purple,
dandelions and violets bask so bright
in the breeze that smells of fresh grass
and cavorts to ruffle our hair, kiss our lips,
when we must stand
here?

How dare all creation exude bright hope
in that terrible hour when we must stand
looking down
the deep, dark walls
of your new grave?

46

HARSH WORLD BEAUTY

Fuck you bitch states Impatient youth,
walking by tall, cocky, proud:

(long tall proud sore swollen full flesh;
cocky cock crow since long ago dawn.)

Echoes down forever of female time,
timeless young demeanor, old definition.

Many-seasoned woman bends
to ancient, ancient task,

inserts impatiens petiole
in warm Mother Earth,

Her moist, shady, dark,
protected place.

Old woman murmurs,
Oh yes, fuck you,
impatient young fools.

Fuck you: insert,
to plant, as a seed,
to plant precious petiole

in warm, shady, moist ground,
warm, dark, earth, here,

warm, dark, moist place
in Old Mother Earth.

Old Mother cuddles all fucked-in
plants. All fucked-up,

these young, living stalks,
now Earth grounded,

Grow
delicate, beautiful blossoms.

48

PICTURE POSTCARD

Greetings from Athens
home of Hera the goddess
whose story we forgot.

When we were lovers we sang
and laughed, reckless together.
Long ago. Seems like yesterday.

This week I visited
truly enduring places
thinking of our old times.

Of late, ancestral ghosts rest
their infinite weight in my belly
invisible hands on my faded crown.

Their voices thin as needles
stitch memories of a self-
directed life. They say

My lessons are not done
the hardest test soon due
leave behind the # 2 pencil.

How I always sweated for freedom.
Writing today from chilly temple ruins.
Wish you were here.

WELL SEASONED

The world ate me up for breakfast
popped me in whole, chewed me to bits,
smacked its lips and spit out my bones,
because I was a sweet young thing.

Obscure and alone on the world's scrap heap,
I knitted joints and tendons,
and stretched on some strands of muscle.

When the world buttered me up for dinner,
popped me in, and bit down to chew,
it quit right quick, left me unscathed,
'cause I'd become a tough old bird.

IT

You came to the game
fragile and undefined
under the tangled, grown-up
canopy of rules and tricks.

I see you hide-and-seeking
behind that wild paisley scarf
of youth, running for "home free!"
before you're tagged.

Any moment you'll find yourself
caught. Mature. Elder.
It. Without a teacher.
Your turn to be wise.

DRESS-SOCKS

husband lost to tv,
kids all self-involved,
job dead-end and boring,
she thought she might just
take the Path of Plath

but first she had to
bring in the dog,
feed the cats,
pack five lunches,
do ten loads of laundry,
clean three bathrooms,
four bedrooms,
and the basement,
change an orthodontist appointment,
correct and get credit on two billing statement
AND
find everyone clean dress-socks
for the funeral.

Clearly, in this household,
there will never, ever, be enough
matched clean dress-socks.

I PERCEIVE THAT MAMA WAS RIGHT

This morning I kneel
to thoroughly clean
the toilet

(cleaner designed for the job
rubber gloves
throw-away scrubbie)

remember
kneeling in my girlhood
for the daily

ten minute prayer
that was part of family worship
kneeling at Wednesday prayer-

meeting at church
for Sunday prayers
and kneeling

at everyday chores
like cleaning the toilet
without accessories

bare hands
an old rag
lye soap

that Mama made
and we used
to wash everything—
clothes
dishes
bodies—

how I saw advertisements
for Tide and Ivory Soap
in Mama's *Lady's Home Companion*

how I first experienced it
at a sleepover
with an English (not Plain)

schoolmate whose family lived
in a brand-new fifties ranch house
and used that floating bath soap

in their pink bathroom how I found it all
scented, amazing, tempting
and frightening.

I remember pondering
even then
the Mary-Martha teaching

how Martha worked
to organize the household
create the feast, earn a living

while Mary sat at Jesus' feet
listening, worshiping, dreaming
not helping with chores

how Martha told Mary, *Come help*,
and Jesus corrected Martha saying, *Mary
has chosen the better part.*

Privileged Mary.
Not like me, born into a family
who worshiped by offering work

with a Mother who taught
that even when I knelt by the toilet
I should also be at prayer

thankful for all—
including the toilet, and I am—
never distinguishing

by what I liked or did not like
for that was the nature
of real love, giving all, and freely.

Again this morning
in my comfortable modern life
I think of Mary, Martha, and Mama.

I perceive that Mama was right.
I still don't understand.

AFTER THE CHOICE

One summer day at the grocery store.

Ripe Bing cherries, mounded in boxes,
glorious burgundy, stems on,
ninety-eight cents per pound.

My hurried hands spread across fruit
in long-known movements,

once used as I picked up eggs
from the grading tray,

eyes quick-checking
before the first touch
and
after the choice,

Now I scan fruit
for mar or rot;

Then I scanned eggs
for cracks, flaws and dirt,
three in each hand, careful
but quick, pack point down.

Home on the farm in the cherry tree—
Oxheart that Grandpa grafted to Black—
Standing sway on my sturdy branch,
I stretched
and picked cherries one at a time,
golden fruit, rose-glow cheeks,
fresh among tooth-edged, simple leaves,

I listened
to warbler tune and insect drum
and wished
I could gather cherries by the handfuls.

In chilly, florescent-lit space
I gather cherries by the handfuls.

WHAT A PICTURE SHOWS

after the photograph "Bending Tree" by Joseph Hyde

Oh look! How the tree leans,
how the sun's dirty, nervous light
glints through heavy clouds.
Color film would have shown
that fearsome greenish tinge
that appears in the sky
just before a tornado.

No. Look again.
Snow scrims the ground.
Twigs ray out as they've grown
on the bending tree and all
the straight background trees.
There is no vast wind.

The burden of dread
does not rest
in the limbs and heart
of the tree.

BROKEN

We crept
through the night
east over mountains
until predawn hours

when we slept.
Slashes of sunlight
across the far range
drew us awake, bleary.

We propped each other,
sighed, tipped the world
to our injured essence,
drank deep,

a heady, healing draught
because in the earthen bowl
before us,
the desert bloomed.

INTERLUDE

WHERE I SET THE BUCKETS DOWN

Groceries in blue bags,
their flesh-cutting weight
pulls my shoulders, bumps my calves,
evokes a clear, sharp memory

of when my arms stretched to balance
the weight of two full milk buckets,
when I squared my shoulders and walked
very tall in order to walk at all.

To reach the milkhouse
where we strained the milk, I counted
each step essential of itself. I walked
the aisle of Holstein tails and rumps,

focused on the clean white door,
its creaky swing and the last three steps
in a whitewashed room
where I set the buckets down,

where I blinked
at the salt sting of victory.

IV

HOME

BORDER KEEP

*keep: to preserve, maintain, hold; to take heed, to notice; a
stronghold, prison, fortress, castle...*

at the edge of day, within
the boundaries I hold
in my hand, this

lovely sculpted being
fine grained wood
worn silk-smooth
head leans slightly forward
graceful arm reaches out

circles worlds
yet embraces nothing
not even warm air
for her left arm
broke
years ago

A FOOT IN EACH WORLD

If awakening years occur in one clay,
if loved ones stay there,
names carved in stone,
that place becomes our permanent home.
All future homes are two and more.

I stand with a foot in two worlds,
the span over memory shards.
Winds shake me, I tremble and shiver,
I've learned to fear free-fall,
and yet
I seek and reach to embrace the power
that pulls me loose, rips me from familiar
place, through time and space

I fly
to my home,
to my home

MOSAIC OF EVERBLUE
One glass vase
cobalt blue
slips from
cold hands
falls on tile.

motherdon'tleaveme!

Shattered
sharp new shapes
scatter
glitter on white
blueness intact.

DANDELION GREENS FOR SUPPER

to fill this hungering
loneliness so deep
that nothing reaches
but breath, pulse
pacing step

colts prance the high meadow
across the hard road between
us, nothing separates
foal and mare

no youngster, I
recall pot pie, apple pie
dandelions' first green
sprigs gathered, cleaned, trimmed
wilted in hot bacon dressing

Mother made

known to us the flowers
of the field, the rippling stream
garden plants, rake and spade

millions of stars visible
to the naked gaze
and I

wish for
I AM
Mother

CENTENARY

This is the day
my mother was born,
one hundred years ago.

She last called me
by name
thirty years ago.

I still hear her
instructions.
I still don't always listen.

SISTER

You're the purebred;
I'm the mutt.
You shared high tea with the Queen;
I romped at the creek, tumbled in.

At school you caught
each proper nuance,
sat with hips even,
back straight, head high,
persistent, obedient
to the end of the course.

I jumped into laps,
nose-nuzzled cheeks,
strayed off course
and stayed in stride
beside a beloved.

You mastered fine arts
and now you paint portraits,
delicate, detailed masterpieces,
and weave gorgeous tapestries.

I found crafts
and now I fingerprint lollipop trees
with the kids, using wash-off paints,
and sew crazy quilts.

Yet as our days parade
your slender, graceful hand

72

and my broad, blunt one
clasp, fingers twined, cling
together.

PAPA'S HANDS

Papa's large hands, long fingers
graceful, sure in his routines,
brown from sun and age,
white marked
where cuts and tears once caused him pain
of which he no longer spoke.

The last time he saw me cry
I stood apart from him,
my head drooped forward,
hair hung straight beside my cheeks
like silk to cover shame.

Then I saw
his high-topped leather work shoes
step within reach
and felt the slightly awkward tug
of my loose strands caught on his calluses.

When I stood on Cemetery Hill
among grass blades that bowed
to wild-grown strawberries,
their sweetness encased in red,
and looked from the polished oak
over Papa's hands
to sturdy Blue Ridge shoulders,

for the first and only time in my life
I saw the mountain move.

LIGHT
following Papa and Mama: Samuel and Naomi,
who always reached for agape love
and wouldn't they be astonished

See the candle flame
so bright, warm and calm

two on each of five folding tables
borrowed from church
covered with white
table paper

candles
and a vase of flowers, centered
on each table set for ten
with silverware, water cups, napkins,

plates stacked next to the food, a buffet
spread on oak deacon-bench tables
that line one wall, covered
with delicious bounty

in the basement
with a wood-stove fire glowing
at the end of the room opposite
steps, steep and narrow enough,

forty eight gathered
siblings, spouses, offspring,
three generations
aged two to seventy seven

stand in a large circle,
bow our heads for the preacher
to invoke the Dear Heavenly Father
to bless us in Jesus' name

then sing
a cappella
in glorious, four part
harmony,

Praise God from whom all blessings flow
Praise Him all creatures here below
Praise Him above ye heavenly host
Praise Father, Son, and Holy Ghost.
                    Amen.

And while we sing:

one son shelters under his arm
the Jewish girl among us;

one daughter
of the newly bankrupt couple
looks at the floor, blond hair
swung forward hiding her face;

one recently divorced clenches
his hands, white knuckled,
and we observe without comment
the absence of his wife and children;

tears mark the cheeks of one
who grieves her dear old horse
put down two weeks ago today
while we all continue

to mourn this anniversary
of the death of our beloved
one who died too young
sister-in-law, aunt, grandmother,
mother, wife;

one savors success—
new degree, new job—
and together we review the roots
from which he grew.

Then my sister, the hostess,
releases the reins of organization
allowing the day to flow
forward, as it will

as we celebrate
enduring, ephemeral ties.

See the candle.
Be the candle.

REGULAR THIEVERY

Summer downpours dumped suddenly as if
to surprise us, as if humanity could be

shocked sane by dousings
like caterwauling cats or mating dogs.

Now gulleys in the lane need smoothing.
I pry up one large, dark stone,

lift it two-handed, prideful,
as if it is my right to take.

There lies a five-lined skink
exposed in its home in moist soil

until now roofed over
by this rock I hold.

I claim a skink's roof as others
claimed for me each part of my house,

took elements from land,
air, and water, as we all do,

and who considers
our regular, everyday thievery.

WARM SUNSHINE CHANGES

Dirt streaks line my window
as if they were icicles, eave-hung
to melt away in the sun

with no effort on my part.
Life is not so
forgiving and simple

as frozen droplet lines
shrunk then disappeared
in warm sunshine changes

nor easy as sooty marks
that wash and polish away
to clear, fresh views.

Life marks etched
in buttocks, belly, breast,
hand, face, eye

time's tracings drawn
in flesh hold mementos
of shadow and light.

LAST CHECK OUTDOORS BEFORE BED

It's me, Pop, your baker's dozen kid.
You up there in them stars?
Soon Spring. Smell it?

Jet here knows, good old dog,
grizzled, gimpy, restless again, like me.

Snow's melting, a relief, looks like
a map in the woods, giving up tracks,
melt and twig-fall scratchings, lines

like some biography writer makes, desk jockey
who never faced terror in war mud, reshaping
our history that most already forgot.

Must get after this poison
ivy, sprouts like Medusa's snake hair.
Hard to keep up these past couple years.

Paperhanger here today, yammered on
how his helper, his born 'n raised kid
turned outlaw, got jailed, so he hired

some chippy to pinch-hit, didn't work,
guy moaned how you can't trust
none but your own. Reg'lar soap opera.

Paper looks good, though. Won't tell Lydia;
compliments give 'er a swelled head.

80

She's pulled out pieces for another scrap
quilt for Joey's little Abby.
Better not buy any more, I tell 'er.

You know, thirteen's turned out pretty lucky
for me. You up there in that starry spangle?
Save a space. I'll be there soon.

THAT PLACE CALLED HOME

After I scrubbed all
the sinks and showers
and floors at least twice,

hung the stock pots,
the clocks, drapes, paintings
and other wall art as usual

I began to imagine
the wallboard, joists, rafters,
asphalt roof and sky-reaching trees

held the aura to suit us
forever, a place of comfort
to fit like old clothes,

in spite of a small, nameless urge
to hunt again for some other place
called home.

BUILD STRONG, SAFE PLACES

warm, wide, centered
between two heartbeats
in that limitless blue
pause

where old joys renew
at still point rest
within the spin of the world
through time

FAMILY REUNION

Tall chicory and Queen Anne's lace
grow side-by-side by summer's road.
Puffy cumulus clouds decorate
bright mid-day skies.

Chubby untanned legs pump,
sparkling eyes invite Grandpa
to lift encircling arms
to play *so big!* games.

Rise and flow and swirl of day,
wading pool, walking shorts, circle
talk elicits advice, shared
pain dissolves in mirth.

Voices lift, unite in song, bless the meal;
fragile blue-veined hands tremble passing
air light angel food cake
on delicate blue willow plates.

V

PRAISE

CIRCLES

We are linked beyond knowing
in our crippled, stumbling ways.

Portraits show us tangled,
grouped as blooms and leaves.

If I am barren
others shall sire and bear.

If I must creep
others shall stride.

If I am silent
others shall speak

Our simple story,
clear words telling

Grace and hope
and how we are

Linked circles,
perfect enough, each

with and in
circles beyond.

SCENT OF SEASONS

At the house in our six-acre woods,
leaves fall in lazy turns,
sensuous
on still air. Each says "shush"
when it lands with others of its kind
already fallen.

I'm stacking firewood, not ours sacrificed,
but purchased, brought on a dump truck, tumbled
in a heap on gravel by the deck,
slab-wood leavings after the sawmill sliced
beams and boards from straight-grown trunks.

Uncured willy-nilly jumble, it exudes
a tangy-sweet scent
everywhere recognized—
the scent of seasons,
tree-life wet in pores and cells,
in every fiber, chunk and sliver,
life sacrificed
to shelter and warmth, those blessed human comforts.

A light and musky presence, the scents
of fresh-cut wood, leaves, and earth,
smells as rich as sustaining stews browned
with onions, simmered with herbs.

I lift, carry, place each piece, with thanks
and reverence for sacrifice and blessing.

TASTE OF A DEEPER RAINBOW

some necessary mourning—
hours, days, years—falls
as a drape across a window
drawn without intention
until a gradual shift begins
the release

and you start to open
again in a world
where marquees and trees
costumes and cloud plumes
now appear to hold more
subtle, dusky colors

NOTE

I wait
for something
deeply thoughtful
maybe profound
for me to say.

What comes
is ordinary quiet.

So I tell you:
In my heart I often
sit with you for a time
in ordinary quiet.

SURVIVORS

The most dazzling creeks
tumble on rocks,
they dance, glitter, and sing.

The most resplendent sunsets
transform clouds
to silver, crimson, and gold.

The most perfected lives,
kiln-fired by sorrow,
grow tender, gracious, serene.

HOMEMADE, EVERYDAY POEMS

I wear my homemade, everyday poems

    like a second skin
        with sturdy lines
        designed to sustain my core

    like a favorite shirt
        made of homespun yarns
        woven on looms of memory

    like a patchwork vest
        some parts straight grain
        some bias

    like a nubby sweater
        knit from a skein of thought

each one carefully shaped and crafted
for warmth and durable comfort.

HER HERITAGE THREADS THROUGH IT

Stars peek through leaves
and the woodland pathway lies dappled
under mysterious shadow weavings.

In the house, a nightlight shines
over simple, minimal furnishings,
complexity hidden
in the handstitched seams
of a patchwork piecing, a unique design
made of odd shapes, multi-colored fabric
scraps of a life unknown. Layered, tied,
bound, remnants of a past creative spirit

blanket this one who now breathes
deep in hard-earned sleep,
infant resting on her breast,
her own scrap piecing in process,
pending a future when her story, too,
blends into the soft, worn composite.

LESSON

Fingers of pain massage
your flesh, your gut, your skull,
even your ear lobes sting.

You want to curl, but this time
you remember, you open
your arms, wide. You find yourself

prone in the cold
as if to make snow angels
but there is only grass.

The whole world's misery
shocks you from crown to sole.
Your suddenly joyful soul shouts

out loud, *Oh, yes! God, it hurts!*
I accept it all, I embrace all life
experience, have compassion;

I know, now, how the whole world is
my sister, my brother, my father, my mother;
I accept the conditions of life. The suffering

dissolves; the only sound in your ear
is the surf, or maybe it's the wind
that catches your breath

or the trumpeting
of the wingéd work
elephant on your chest.

And then
your broken heart
will set you free.

FROM A WARM, EMPTY ROOM

I admit to the truth and un-
truth of everything that is

> and none of it matters
> nothing matters

even your father's craziness
and your sister's death don't matter

> *nothing* matters
> *and everything* matters

it *all* matters

every bit of your experience
and mine   our singular
presence in the world

every breath   every sunrise
and noontime and midnight
noticed or not

every kiss   every swing of hair
every raccoon and sparrow
and raindrop in the world

every butterfly wing stroke

just whispering

96

HOW TO ACCEPT THE GIFT

The twins, boredom and depression,
hold hands and skip along your river path
say, *Here we are! We will ride your back
for a while.* Through daily steps,

slept-through, sleepless times of fever, lassitude,
pain: physical, emotional, spiritual—
the common bonds, the common divides—
you stretch, long, heavy, fragile,

balanced on the rim of somewhere else
like a leaf on the edge at the waterfall,
no turning back, no escape, no pill
that will clear the ills and murk

and you must turn and say to your specific,
aching, encasing muscles and skin,
*What kind of pain, exactly? Sharp, achy,
smooth and continuous, pulsing, weepy?*

And you must explore the weight
that covers you like a lead body suit
that you cannot unzip and shed,
And you must find an inner cauldron

where you will hold that excess heat,
chill, and constancy, and say, *This too,
this too,* and in that container the thought
of unbearable becomes unrecognizable,

(Of course. You bear your life as given
as long as breath comes, and fair
is only a summer event in small towns
with a Ferris wheel and a big tent.)

And you will find beauty, joy and delight,
finally, anyway, in the flavors of light
in days and nights, in faces, shoulders, thighs
of all who help you rise, and bathe,

who bring their whirlwind, and their own
honest misery, reverence, laughter and fear,
tears and the carrying of the twins and all,
And finally you turn with an eager shout. *Yes!*

WE PAUSE TO GIVE THANKS

For the voyage of life from seed to harvest, the kiss
of rain and sun and growth, the gifts of the earth given

Into the hands of strangers, friends and family
whose efforts now bring such bounty to this table.

Thanks for the soft animal body that carries each life
here present, so sturdy and so fragile;

Thanks and praise for fellowship, and for the lives
of those now absent whose essence lingers among us;

Thanks for the complex ways we each continue to seek
and find our place, unique like everyone else.

Lead us to the gift of regular silence until it silences us;
bring us to choose gratitude until we are truly grateful;

Fill us with praise until we ourselves become
a constant act of praise.

So we give thanks for all things, including joys
and sorrows deeply felt but left, here, unspoken.

WINTER LIGHTS

The sun sets through its glory of color and night settles.
I observe the shifting splendor only in glances
through a polished window from where I work
at a gray machine, the egg grader, motor whirring

those winters of my early teens, home on the farm,
our nearest neighbor half-a-mile by field.

Chores complete, I turn out all the lights.
Sometimes the barn is dark, too, and I am the last one done.
I blindly step from the chicken house onto the lovely ground.

My young eyes adjust, I am safe
in the clear night, in the crisp air
on a known and trusted path

under that navy-black sky so thick with stars it seems like the
misty spray of a huge but silent waterfall
flung, white, across the sky.

I, alone, am mistress of my small and limitless universe.

In the kitchen, two ceiling bulbs burn, and fire in the stove.
Mama, Papa and one sister wait. Supper is on the table.

FINALE

INHERITED ESTATE

Night storms and pain give way
to bright morning rush;

The cat meows for breakfast,
curls on his perch for a nap;

Faucets gush, the vacuum sings,
the breeze blows clear and clean.

Fresh baked honey-wheat bread
perfumes a warm noon kitchen;

Clean dry sheets taut on the beds
hold smells of today's sunshine;

A chat on the phone with a friend;
a book, a tender family. Miles away

at the unused homestead barn, a wing
of the roof folds down on broken rafters.

Westering brilliance uplights strong
young oaks, ash, a trio of cedars;

We stand together on the rim of the hill
bearing witness

AFTERWORD

In 1972 Carol Bross, now Bindel, came to my office at Iowa State University to say she would like me to be her major professor for her master's degree

I asked about her experiences and interests. She seemed confident and in control of her goals. I accepted and soon learned she was a fine writer as she enthusiastically demonstrated in her terms papers for my classes. But that came out even more clearly when she began her thesis.

She knew her topic and wrote about it creatively. I was so impressed that I hoped she would continue for a doctoral degree but she had things to do, places to go, and goals to accomplish. For one thing, she had married by then and had to make decisions jointly with her husband Bernard Bindel.

Years passed, my wife and I kept in contact with her and her husband, exchanging cards, letter, e-mails, and infrequent visits. From time to time she sent us a copy of something she had written, poetry more than anything. Every now and again she sent news about a poem that had been published. Meantime, I and my wife developed a small publishing business in which we publish the poetry and fiction of new writers

As her writing record built up I began to think she might want to put her work into book form and offered to publish it. When I received her poem called Light, I knew for sure that here was something special. Her marvelous understanding of family, nature, and how they intertwine arose from her life as the youngest of a dozen or so children. A childhood in a devoutly religious farm family followed by education, a career of hard work, and the raising of three genius sons, produced a creative, sensitive artist with one foot in her (extended as well as nuclear) family's ideas about life and one foot in her own special version.

She is the mother of three grown sons and lives quietly with her husband in rural Maryland. The trees, the rolling hills, the neighboring farms and forests provide the gentlest of surroundings for her daily walks that inform and give rise to her poetry.

The front cover photo of the family farm where Carol and her siblings grew up was taken by Carol's sister, Ruth, a member of the photo club in her high school in the 1950s. The photo shows the summer house/smokehouse, part of the house itself, and all the out-buildings, (even the old out house!).

The big chicken house was built only a few months before. It wasn't painted yet, just raw cement blocks. The old summer house/smoke house burned not long after the photo was taken.

The willow tree that towers over the house was planted when Carol was newborn. It eventually had to be cut down, its roots having grown into the septic system. In the photo above Carol and a sister play in the nearby creek.

After many e-mail messages back and forth we agreed publishing a book of her poetry was thing to do. We three, Carol, Mary Winter and I met at Carol's house for four days formatting the book, after Carol and Dana Knighten chose the poems and arranged the order. The result is this volume of Carol Bindel's wonderful poetry. We are pleased to be have been permitted to present such high quality work.

I want to thank several people for their help without which my job as publisher would have been difficult. First, to Bernie Bindel for all he did to facilitate Carol's and my work and to Mary Winter for various helpful deeds but especially her help with the IT work and for the careful copy editing. At Chapbook Press the help of Pierre Camy and Bill Chesney was crucial to getting the book through the system.

Earl W. Morris

CITATIONS

I thank the editors of the following publications in which some of the poems have previously appeared, sometimes in slightly different form.

Artistic License: Pond Bottom Stone, The Idea, Love Like Water

Baltimore City Paper: Explore Beyond; Rooms of Time

From the Front Porch: Pond Bottom Stone

Late Knocking Earth Journey Pond Bottom Stone

Loch Raven Review: Winter Lights

Manorborn: Picture Postcard; After the Choice

The Gunpowder Review: How to Find Your Poem

The Harford Poet: Perfect Secrets; Family Reunion; Papa's Hands

The Pen Woman: Survivors

Time of Singing:Survivors

UUFHC Newsletter: Papa's Hands; Light; Winter Lights

Welter: How to Accept the Gift